H(

In this boo|
will develo|

SPEAKER

by talking
by prepari:

READERS

by reading
by looking

WRITERS

by writing
by writing your own poems

Learning Zone

Please return this book to the Learning Zone on or before the date shown below. Thank you.

At different stages, you will write as a war reporter for a newspaper. Make a note-book for these pieces of writing. Turn the page to read the first poems about war …

TO FIGHT OR NOT TO FIGHT?

Many poets, male and female, have chosen to write about war. Thousands of poems were written about the First World War (1914–18). Many more were written about the Second World War (1939–45), especially **the Holocaust** and the dropping of the first atomic bombs.

More recently, poets have written about fighting in Vietnam, Iraq and Bosnia.

People often view war in different ways. Some support it while others deeply disagree with it.

> **GLOSSARY**
>
> **the Holocaust** – the word for Germany's attempt to wipe out the Jews in the Second World War.

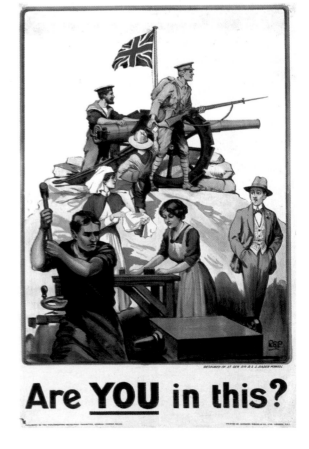

Recruitment material for the First World War

Read the following three poems. They all have different views of war.

OH STAY AT HOME, MY LAD, AND PLOUGH

Oh stay at home, my lad, and plough
The land and not the sea,
And leave the soldiers at their **drill**,
And all about the **idle** hill
Shepherd your sheep with me.

Oh stay with company and **mirth**
And daylight and the air;
Too full already is the grave
Of **fellows** that were good and brave
And died because they were.

A. E. Housman

> ## GLOSSARY
>
> **drill** – training exercises for soldiers
>
> **idle** – peaceful, unoccupied
>
> **mirth** – laughter, fun
>
> **fellows** – men

HEART OF OAK (extract)

Come, cheer up, my lads! 'tis to glory we steer,
To add something more to this wonderful year;
To honour we call you, not **press** you like slaves –
For who are so free as we sons of the waves?
   Heart of **oak** are our ships,
   Heart of oak are our men;
   We always are ready;
   Steady, boys, steady;
We'll fight and we'll conquer again and again.

David Garrick

> ## GLOSSARY
>
> **press** – press-gang, force someone to join the navy
>
> **oak** – wood from the oak tree, known to be very hard

FOR TWO VOICES

'O mother, mother, isn't it fun,
The soldiers marching past in the sun!'
'Child, child, what are you saying?
Come to church. We should be praying.'

'Look, mother, at their bright spears!'
'The leaves are falling like women's tears.'
'You are not looking at what I see.'
'**Nay**, but I look at what must be.'

'Hark to the **pipers**! See the flags flying!'
'I hear the sound of a girl crying.'
'How many hundreds before they are **done**?'
'How many mothers **wanting** a son?'

'Here rides the general, pacing slow!'
'Well he may, if he knows what I know.'
'O this war, what a glorious game!'
'Sin and shame, sin and shame.'

Maurice Hewlett August 1914

GLOSSARY

nay – no

pipers – players of bagpipes

done – finished

wanting – lacking

- Who do you think is advising the 'lad' in Housman's poem? What advice is given to him?

- What is the poet's view of war in 'Heart of Oak'?

- Make a copy of 'For Two Voices'. Highlight the lines spoken by the child. What is his view of the soldiers? Highlight in a different colour the lines spoken by the mother. How is her view different?

- In a pair, work out a reading of either 'Heart of Oak' or 'For Two Voices'. Record it. Play it to the rest of the class. Say what effect you were aiming at.

- Write a paragraph about each of the poems. Explain what view of war is presented by each poet. Add a fourth paragraph explaining your own thoughts about war.

THE CHARGE OF THE LIGHT BRIGADE

Fighting in battle can lead to great acts of bravery. Many soldiers have been given medals for what they have done. Sometimes they have lived to tell their story. Sometimes they have died.

Soldiers are trained to carry out the orders given to them by their leaders. Some famous mistakes have been made. These have led to the death of many men.

One of the best-known errors happened in the Crimean War. Britain and France were fighting Russia.

In October, 1854, the Russians attacked the British at Balaclava, in an area of Russia known as the Crimea.

The commander had not understood his orders. He was supposed to order his men to capture some Russian guns. Instead, he ordered them to charge the main Russian position, riding on horses. Six-hundred men rode into the 'valley of death'. One-hundred and thirteen were killed and 134 wounded. Five-hundred horses lost their lives.

THE CHARGE OF THE LIGHT BRIGADE

I

Half a **league**, half a league,
  Half a league onward,
All in the valley of Death
  Rode the six hundred.
'Forward, the Light Brigade!
Charge for the guns!' he said:
Into the valley of Death
  Rode the six hundred.

II

'Forward, the Light Brigade!'
Was there a man dismayed?
Not though the soldier knew
  Some one had **blundered**:
Theirs not to make reply,
Theirs not to reason why,
Theirs but to do and die:
Into the valley of Death
  Rode the six hundred.

III

Cannon to right of them,
Cannon to left of them,
Cannon in front of them
  Volleyed and thundered;
Stormed at with shot and shell,
Boldly they rode and well,
Into the jaws of Death,
Into the mouth of Hell
  Rode the six hundred.

IV

Flashed all their **sabres** bare,
Flashed as they turned in air
Sabring the gunners there,
Charging an army, while
  All the world wondered:
Plunged in the **battery-smoke**
Right through the line they broke;
Cossack and Russian
Reeled from the sabre-stroke
  Shattered and **sundered**.
Then they rode back, but not
  Not the six hundred.

V

Cannon to right of them,
Cannon to left of them,
Cannon behind them
  Volleyed and thundered;
Stormed at with shot and shell,
While horse and hero fell,
They that had fought so well
Came through the jaws of Death,
Back from the mouth of Hell,
All that was left of them,
  Left of six hundred.

VI

When can their glory fade?
O the wild charge they made!
  All the world wondered.
Honour the charge they made!
Honour the Light Brigade,
  Noble six hundred!

Alfred Tennyson

GLOSSARY

league – about three miles

blundered – made a mistake

volleyed – fired at the same time

sabres – sword with curved blade

battery-smoke – smoke from the guns

Cossack – a person from south-eastern Russia or a horse used by the Russian army

sundered – broken apart

honour – respect

- Look at stanzas I and II. Make a list of words which tell you something terrible is about to take place.

- The main events of the poem are described in stanzas III, IV and V. Produce a flow diagram about these three stanzas. Explain what happens to the British brigade in each stanza. Start:

Cannons fire on all sides

↓

They continue charging

↓

- Look at the last stanza. What is Tennyson's view of the charge?

- 'Theirs not to make reply, Theirs not to reason why, Theirs but to do and die'. Tennyson thinks soldiers should simply obey orders. Discuss this in a small group. Should soldiers always do what they are told?

HELP

A **stanza** of poetry is a group of lines set out by themselves. Sometimes people call this a verse of poetry.

Charge of the Light Brigade, Balaclava, 25 October 1854

After the charge

WAR REPORTER – 1

This is the first of the two times you will write as a war reporter. You are a reporter for *The Times* newspaper. You are in the Crimea. You watched the charge from a distance.

You talk to three of the surviving soldiers after the battle. Two of them see the charge as a brave, glorious defeat. One is very upset about their leader's blunder. Write down their comments in your note-book.

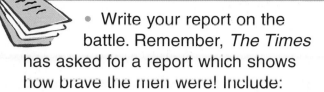

• Write your report on the battle. Remember, *The Times* has asked for a report which shows how brave the men were! Include:

1 A headline

2 A report on what happened. This could begin: 'At ten minutes past eleven this morning, our Light Cavalry Brigade advanced…'

3 Some comments from the interviews you carried out. This could begin 'Survivors told me…'

4 Your own view of the charge. This could begin 'As an observer, I can say…'

The Times

1d   26 October 1854

Headline

At ten minutes past eleven this morning, our Light Cavalry Brigade advanced

THE FIRST WORLD WAR (1914–18)

TRAINING

In the First World War new soldiers had to learn how to use their bayonets. This was the sharp blade fixed to the end of their guns. They would practise by attacking sacks of straw. These would be hung in the air or put on the ground.

The sergeant who trained the men tried to make them 'put on the killing face'. This was meant to terrify the enemy still more.

This is an extract from a training book used in the First World War:

> **Vulnerable Parts of the Body** – If possible, the point of the bayonet should be directed against an opponent's throat, especially in man to man fighting, as the point will enter easily and make a fatal wound on penetrating a few inches and, being near the eyes, makes an opponent **funk**. Other vulnerable and usually exposed parts are the face, chest, lower abdomen and thighs, and the region of the kidneys when the back is turned. Four to six inches penetration is enough to **incapacitate** and allow for a quick withdrawal, whereas, if a bayonet is driven home too far it is often impossible to withdraw it. In such cases a shot should be fired to break up the obstruction.

GLOSSARY

vulnerable – part of the body that can be wounded

funk – be very afraid

incapacitate – kill or seriously wound

- What is the writer's view of killing people?
- How did you feel when you read these instructions? Why?
- What words does the writer use to avoid saying the victim is a real person?

BAYONET TRAINING

From far away, a mile or so,
The wooden **scaffolds** could be seen
On which fat **felons** swung;
But closer view showed these to be
Sacks, **corpulent** with straw and tied
To beams from which they hung.

The sergeant halted his platoon.
'Right lads,' he barked, 'you see them sacks?
I want you to forget
That sacks is what they are and act
As if they was all **Jerries** – wait!
Don't move a muscle yet!

'I'm going to show you how to use
The bayonet as it should be done.
If any of you feel
Squeamish like, I'll tell you this:
There's one thing Jerry just can't face
And that thing is cold steel.

'So if we're going to win this war
You've got to understand you must
Be brutal, ruthless, tough.
I want to hear you scream for blood
As you rip out his guts and see
The stuff he had for **duff**.

'All right? Platoon, in your own time,
Fix your bayonets; stand at ease
Then watch my moves with care.
First, the High Port, done like this:
You **cant** the rifle straight across
Your chest and hold it there.

'Note the angle: left hand firm
Around the barrel, half-way down.
The right hand grasps the small.
Whatever happens never change
Your grip upon your weapon. No!
I don't mean that at all!

'You dirty-minded little sods!
The next position – that's On Guard –
You swing the bayonet out
In front of you like this, chest high,
Take one pace forward with your left
Knee bent. Let's see you try.

'High Port! On Guard! High Port! On Guard!
All right. You've got the rough idea.
Stand easy and keep still.
And now – Delivery of the Point –
In other words the moment when
You go in for the kill.

'So watch me now and listen good.
I'll want to hear you yell like me,
So take a good deep breath
Before you stick the bayonet in.
If you don't kill him with the blade
You'll scare the sod to death!'

The young recruits stood there and watched
And listened as their tutor roared
And stabbed his lifeless foe;
Their faces were expressionless,
Impassive as the winter skies
Black with threats of snow.

Vernon Scannell

GLOSSARY

scaffold – platform used for hanging people

felons – criminals

corpulent – fat

Jerries – Germans

duff – dinner

cant – move

impassive – without feeling

HELP

Simile – when a poet compares something with something else. A simile uses 'like' or 'as'. For example, the fields looked **like** a patchwork quilt.

Quotations – when you use some actual words from a poem, this is called a quotation. Quoted words are put in speech marks. For example, the sergeant tells the soldiers to act as if the sacks of straw were 'Jerries'.

- Look at the first stanza which tells you about where the training is taking place. Use the information to sketch the training equipment.

- The next eight stanzas describe the training. What can you tell about the sergeant?

- The sergeant wants to make sure the soldiers know how to use a bayonet. Point out the parts of the poem which tell them how to do it. He also wants them to learn to be brutal to the enemy. Point out the bits which teach them to be brutal.

- Look at the last three lines of the poem. What simile does Scannell use to describe the soldiers' faces? What do you think the soldiers might be feeling or thinking?

- Write about the training book and the poem. For each one, write a paragraph about:

    why you think it was written

    who it was written for

    what kinds of words it uses. Include some examples.

Add a paragraph at the end explaining how you felt about each piece of writing and why.

- In pairs, produce a reading of the poem.

OVER THE TOP

Much of the fighting in the First World War made use of trenches. These were long ditches dug in the ground. The trenches stretched for hundreds of miles across France and Belgium.

Each army dug trench systems. There was a special trench leading to the front line. Toilets were dug at the end of short trenches. The front trench was over two metres deep. It was about a metre wide at the bottom.

Small shelters called dug-outs were built in the sides of the trenches. They had iron or wooden rooves. They were covered with earth and sandbags.

The two armies were separated by an area known as 'no man's land'. This was defended with razor-sharp barbed wire. Usually it would be covered with huge shell holes full of mud and water. Sometimes there was only a short distance between the two armies' front lines. You could hear the enemy talking!

One of the most terrifying times was waiting for the order to leave your trench and attack the enemy.

OVER THE TOP

Ten more minutes! – Say yer prayers,
Read yer Bibles – pass the rum!
Ten more minutes! Strike me dumb,
'Ow they creeps on unawares,
Those blooming minutes. Nine. It's queer,
I'm sorter stunned. It ain't with fear!

Eight. It's like as if a frog
Waddled round in your inside,
Cold as ice-blocks, straddle wide,
Tired o' waiting. Where's the **grog**?
Seven. I'll play yer **pitch and toss** –
Six. – I wins, and tails yer loss.

'Nother minute sprinted by
'Fore I knowed it; only Four
(Break 'em into seconds) more
'Twixt us and Eternity.
Every word I've ever said
Seems a-shouting in my head.

Three. Larst night a little star
Fairly shook up in the sky,
Didn't like the lullaby
Rattled by the dogs of War.
Funny thing – that star all white
Saw old **Blighty**, too, larst night.

Two. I ain't ashamed o' prayers,
They're only wishes sent ter God
Bits o' plants from bloody **sod**
Trailing up His golden stairs.
Ninety seconds – Well, who cares!
One –
No **fife**, no **blare**, no drum –
Over the Top – to Kingdom Come!

Sybil Bristowe

GLOSSARY

grog – alcohol such as rum

pitch and toss – a game involving throwing coins

'twixt – between

Blighty – England

sod – the ground, earth

fife – a kind of flute used with drums by armies

blare – sound of a trumpet

- Pick out each mention of time passing. What is the poet trying to tell us about waiting to go over the top?

- The poem gives us the thoughts of the soldier in his own words. Some of the words give us clues about the sort of man he is. In pairs, list the words which tell you how he speaks and where he might come from. Present your findings to other pairs. Do you agree with each other?

- Imagine you are about to go 'over the top'. Write your thoughts as time passes. You might want to write a poem or a description. You could start: 'Only five more minutes to go…'

Going 'over the top'

AT THE FRONT

Read the following two poems:

SUICIDE IN THE TRENCHES

I knew a simple soldier boy
Who grinned at life in empty joy,
Slept soundly through the lonesome dark,
And whistled early with the lark.

In winter trenches, **cowed** and glum,
With **crumps** and **lice** and lack of rum,
He put a bullet through his brain.
No one spoke of him again.

You **smug-faced** crowds with **kindling eye**
Who cheer when soldier lads march by,
Sneak home and pray you'll never know
The hell where youth and laughter go.

Siegfried Sassoon

A DEAD BOCHE

To you who'd read my songs of War
And only hear of blood and fame,
I'll say (you've heard it said before)
'War's Hell!' and if you doubt the same,
Today I found in **Mametz Wood**
A certain cure for **lust** of blood:

Where, propped against a shattered trunk,
In a great mess of things unclean,
Sat a dead Boche; he scowled and stunk
With clothes and face a sodden green,
Big-bellied, spectacled, crop-haired,
Dribbling black blood from nose and beard.

Robert Graves

GLOSSARY

cowed – crouching in fear

crumps – sound of a bursting shell

lice – insects living in hair or on skin

smug-faced – with a self-satisfied expression

kindling eye – bright, glowing, excited eyes

GLOSSARY

Boche – French slang for a German

Mametz Wood – a wood on the banks of the River Somme in France

lust – a strong desire

German corpse, the Somme, November 1916

• Working in a pair, copy and fill in the following grid:

Title of poem	
What the poem is about	
How the poem is organised (e.g. stanzas, rhyme)	
Words or lines you like, and why	

• In your pair, prepare a talk about one of the poems. Make use of the notes you made in the grid. Include:

  – a reading of the poem

  – comments on what the poem is about, how it is organised, parts you liked and why, and your overall view of the poem.

A POET – WILFRED OWEN

Wilfred Owen was one of the most famous First World War poets. He was in France when war broke out. At first he thought the war was a good thing. He trained as an officer. He was sent to fight in France at the end of 1916.

Fighting in the trenches changed his view of the war. After a shell burst near him, he was sent to Craiglockhart Hospital in Scotland. There he was treated for shell-shock.

At the hospital, Owen wrote poems about his terrifying time in France. One of his best-known poems is about a gas attack.

The title of this poem by Wilfred Owen comes from a Roman poet called Horace. He wrote in one of his poems: 'Dulce et decorum est pro patria mori' – it is sweet and right to die for your country.

DULCE ET DECORUM EST

Owen describes a group of very tired soldiers leaving the trenches. They are going away from the front for a break from duty.

Bent double, like old beggars under sacks,
Knock-kneed, coughing like hags, we cursed through sludge,
Till on the haunting **flares** we turned our backs
And towards our distant rest began to trudge.
Men marched asleep. Many had lost their boots
But limped on, blood-shod. All went lame; all blind;
Drunk with fatigue; deaf even to the hoots
Of tired, outstripped **Five-Nines** that dropped behind.

On their way there is a gas attack by the enemy. One man cannot get his mask on in time.

Gas! GAS! Quick, boys! – An **ecstasy of fumbling**,
Fitting the clumsy helmets just in time;
But someone still was yelling out and stumbling,
And flound'ring like a man in fire or **lime**…
Dim, through the misty panes and thick green light,
As under a green sea, I saw him drowning.

Owen cannot stop dreaming about the man's pain.

In all my dreams, before my helpless sight,
He plunges at me, **guttering**, choking, drowning.

Owen has a message for people who believe in war. If they had seen this man's pain, their view of war would change.

If in some smothering dreams you too could pace
Behind the wagon that we flung him in,
And watch the white eyes **writhing** in his face,
His hanging face, like a devil's sick of sin;
If you could hear, at every jolt, the blood
Come gargling from the froth-corrupted lungs,
Obscene as cancer, bitter as the **cud**
Of vile, incurable sores on innocent tongues, –
My friend, you would not tell with such high **zest**
To children **ardent** for some desperate glory,
The old Lie: Dulce et decorum est
Pro patria mori.

Wilfred Owen

[*continued over …*]

GLOSSARY

flares – bright lights used to signal or light up the battle-field

five-nines – types of shell

ecstasy of fumbling – frenzied, awkward movement

lime – sticky, burning substance

guttering – flowing in streams (like wax running down a candle)

writhing – twisting

obscene – repulsive

cud – food chewed for a long time by animals such as cows

zest – excitement, enjoyment

ardent – eager

• Produce a drawing for each stanza of the poem. Make use of the detail Owen gives you.
Choose one or two quotations to go with each drawing.

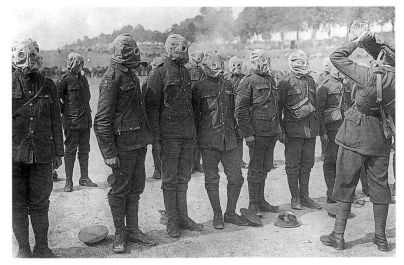

Practice at putting on gas masks

WAR REPORTER – 2

You travel to Craiglockhart Hospital to interview Owen about his fighting in the war. You know he saw a gas attack. Owen has already sent you a copy of 'Dulce'.

- On the train to Scotland you get out your note-book. You write down some questions you want to ask Owen about his poem. Your first questions are:

  1. Did you actually see a gas attack when you were in France?

  2. Why did you describe the soldiers as 'like old beggars under sacks'?

  Write down five other questions in your note-book.

- In pairs, discuss how Owen might answer your questions.

- In your pair, decide who will be the reporter and who will be Owen. Carry out the interview.

- Working alone, write up Owen's answers to the questions. Set it out like this:

  Question 1: *Can I ask whether you saw a gas attack in France?*

  Owen: *Yes, I did. I shall never forget it. I saw what it could do to men. I had to write about it.*

  Question 2: *In the first stanza, why did you…*

Wilfred Owen

DESERTERS

Many soldiers could not cope with the stress. Conditions were terrible. They had to put up with poor food, rats, lice, mud and water. There would be the remains of dead soldiers in the trenches. They were often under attack for long periods of time. The thought of 'going over the top' must have terrified them.

Some soldiers chose to desert. This meant they would disobey orders and run away from the battlefield.

If a deserter was caught, the punishment was usually death by firing squad.

Conditions were terrible

THE DESERTER

There was a man, – don't mind his name,
Whom Fear had dogged by night and day.
He could not face the German guns
And so he turned and ran away.
But who can judge him, you or I?
God makes a man of flesh and blood
Who **yearns** to live and not to die.
And this man when he feared to die
Was scared as any frightened child,
His knees were shaking under him,
His breath came fast, his eyes were wild.
I've seen a hare with eyes as wild,
With throbbing heart and sobbing breath.

But oh! it shames one's soul to see
A man in **abject** fear of death.
But fear had gripped him, so had death;
His number had gone up that day,
They might not **heed** his frightened eyes,
They shot him when the dawn was grey.
Blindfolded, when the dawn was grey,
He stood there in a place apart,
The shots rang out and down he fell,
An English bullet in his heart.
An English bullet in his heart!
But here's the **irony** of life, –
His mother thinks he fought and fell
A hero, foremost in the **strife**.
So she goes proudly; to the strife
Her best, her hero son she gave.
O well for her she does not know
He lies in a deserter's grave.

Winifred Letts

GLOSSARY

yearns – longs to

abject – deeply miserable

heed – take notice of

irony – strange twist

strife – battle

- Look at lines 9–18. List the words or phrases which tell you what sort of state the man is in. What is he compared to in lines 13–14? Why?

- What does the mother think about her son? Why do you think she thinks this?

THE DESERTER

'I'm sorry I done it, Major.'
We bandaged the **livid** face;
And led him out, **ere** the **wan** sun rose,
To die his death of disgrace.

The **bolt-heads** locked to the **cartridge**;
The rifles steadied to rest,
As cold **stock** nestled at colder cheek
And **foresight** lined on the breast.

'Fire!' called the Sergeant-Major.
The **muzzles** flamed as he spoke:
And the shameless soul of a nameless man
Went up in the **cordite**-smoke.

Gilbert Frankau

GLOSSARY

livid – bluish, leaden colour

ere – before

wan – pale

bolt-head, cartridge, stock, foresight, muzzle – all parts of a gun

cordite – smoke from the gun as it is fired

- Which words in the first stanza tell you how the deserter feels?

- What is described in the second stanza? Whose point of view do you get?

- Read the last two lines. What do you think is the poet's view of the deserter and his death?

- Imagine you are a member of the firing squad. Write your diary entry for the day the deserter was shot. Bring out your feelings about what you had to do. You could begin:

'Today I had to do something all soldiers fear. I had to kill one of my own side. It all started just before dawn...'

THE SECOND WORLD WAR (1939–45)

THE BLITZ

The Second World War was fought in a very different way to the First. There was far less trench warfare. There were far more air attacks. Large numbers of bombs were dropped in air raids on enemy cities. Buildings were badly damaged and many people were killed.

Germany tried to bring the war against Britain to a quick end. In the Battle of Britain, German planes tried to bomb Britain into giving up. This was Hitler's 'blitzkrieg' – the German word for a very short, violent war. London was heavily bombed by German planes in what Londoners called 'The Blitz'.

Lois Clark drove a stretcher-party car during the Blitz. She worked in the Clapham and Brixton area of London. Her job was to give first aid at the scene of a bombing. On the next page is a poem she wrote about her work during the Blitz.

PICTURE FROM THE BLITZ

After all these years
I can still close my eyes and see
her sitting there,
in her big armchair,
grotesque under an open sky,
framed by the jagged lines of her broken house.

Sitting there,
a plump homely person,
steel needles still in her work-rough hands;
grey with dust, stiff with shock,
but breathing,
no blood or distorted limbs;
breathing, but stiff with shock,
knitting unravelling on her apron'd knee.

They have taken the stretchers off my car
and I am running
under the **pattering flack**
over a mangled garden;
treading on something soft
and fighting the rising **nausea** –
only a far-flung cushion, bleeding feathers.

They lift her gently
out of her great armchair,
tenderly,
under the open sky,
a shock-frozen woman trailing khaki wool.

Lois Clark

GLOSSARY

grotesque – ugly

pattering flack – the sound of anti-aircraft fire

nausea – feeling of sickness

- Look at the opening three lines. Why is the poem called 'Picture from the Blitz'?

- Use details from the first two stanzas to produce a picture of the scene. Label your picture with some quotations from this part of the poem.

- Which words in the last stanza show how the rescuers treated the shocked woman?

- Write the thoughts of the woman on the armchair after she has come round from the shock. Include:

  what she was doing before the bomb dropped

  her memories of the bomb explosion

  her feelings as she sat in the ruins

  her rescue

  her thoughts about not being killed

  You could begin: 'There I was minding my own business. I was in my living room knitting a pullover for my Ronnie. He's a soldier in Africa, you know. Suddenly…'

THE HOLOCAUST

Part of Germany's plan in the Second World War was to blame Jews for all German troubles. They worked up a hatred of Jews.

Large prison camps were built at places like Auschwitz. Six million Jews died in these camps. Many were gassed to death in buildings which the prisoners thought were shower blocks.

The Holocaust was one of the worst things man has ever done to man.

A soldier clears the corpses of some Holocaust victims

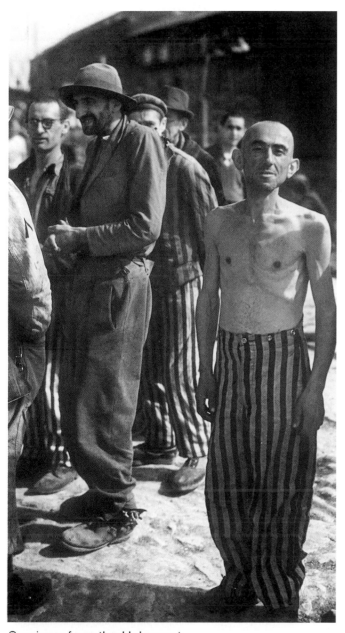

Survivors from the Holocaust

AUSCHWITZ (extract)

What big heavy doors!
Strange, lingering odour,
Faint but still here…strong disinfectant.
'Stand round the shower point.'
Wait for the water. Don't think about the crowd.
They don't notice your **degradation**.
They can't see your shaved head from all the rest!

My God!…They're locking those bloody great doors!
Why?…It can't be!
No, the water will come in a minute.
Don't cry, just be patient,
It will be all over very soon.
There's a noise – up there.
He's lifting that grate.
All eyes watching, wondering.
No sound.
What are those pellets?… Dry disinfectant.
Sulphur!!?

Gas! Gas! Gas! Panic!
The screams, the clutching,
Pulling, scrambling.
The total terror of realisation.

Timeless minutes climbing and scrambling.
Families forgotten. **Self preservation**.
Flesh on flesh – clutching and tearing.
Gas, screams, death…silence.

Elizabeth Wyse

> ### GLOSSARY
>
> **degradation** – lowered self-esteem
>
> **sulphur** – a chemical used to gas people to death
>
> **self preservation** – saving yourself

SHEMA

You who live secure
In your warm houses,
Who return at evening to find
Hot food and friendly faces:

Consider whether this is a man,
Who **labors** in the mud
Who knows no peace
Who fights for a crust of bread
Who dies at a yes or no.
Consider whether this is a woman,
Without hair or name
With no more strength to remember
Eyes empty and womb cold
As a frog in winter.

Consider that this has been:
I **commend** these words to you.
Engrave them on your hearts
When you are in your house,
When you walk on your way,
When you go to bed, when you rise.
Repeat them to your children.
Or may your house crumble,
Disease **render** you powerless,
Your **offspring avert** their faces from you.

Primo Levi, 10 January 1946

Translated from the Italian by Ruth Feldman and Brian Stone

- Look at the first four lines of 'Shema'. Who has Primo Levi written this poem for?

- Look at the second stanza. What sort of suffering did men and women experience in the camps?

- What do you think Levi means by these two lines in the second stanza: 'Consider whether this is a man' and 'Consider whether this is a woman'?

- Read the first six lines of the last stanza. What does the poet want us to do with the words of the poem? Will you?

- Look at the last three lines. What does Levi want to happen to us if we ignore his poem?

- The events of the Holocaust described in these two poems are very frightening. They have also been described in films like *Schindler's List*. There are old films and photos showing the actual camps. It happened only 50 years ago, in living memory. Is it right that people should be reminded about them?

GLOSSARY

labors – works hard (American spelling)

commend – give to someone for safe-keeping

engrave – carve on the surface

render – make

offspring – children

avert – turn away

NUCLEAR WAR

At the end of the Second World War, two atomic bombs were dropped on Japan by the USA. Some say it ended the war and saved lives. Others say it was a terrible crime.

Sixty-thousand people died in the explosion at Hiroshima. Tens of thousands were injured or died later. People still suffer from the effects of radiation.

A nuclear explosion in the Pacific, 1945

FLAMES (extract)

After that concentrated moment
of the explosion,
pure **incandescent** hatred
spreads out, boundless.
Blank silence
piles up into the air.

The hot rays of **uranium**
that shouldered the sun aside
burn onto a girl's back
the flowered pattern of thin silk,
set **instantaneously** ablaze
the black **garb** of the priest –
August 6, 1945:
that midday midnight
man burned the gods
at the stake.
Hiroshima's night of fire
cast its glow over sleeping **humanity**;
before long
history will set an **ambush**
for all who would play God.

Toge Sankichi

Translated from the Japanese by Richard H. Minear

• Re-read the poem. What does it describe?

• Look carefully at the last nine lines. Discuss in pairs what you think they mean. Comment on what the poet thinks about the dropping of the bomb. What does he mean by the last three lines?

Hiroshima after the atomic bomb, August 1945

'Flames' is a very serious poem about the bombing of Hiroshima. Some poets have written about the threat of nuclear war in a more light-hearted way:

IN A BLINDING FLASH

'Ho! ho! that's the best joke I've heard in …
'Come here, let mummy dry your …
'Oh, Howard we can't keep meeting like …
'Hang on lads! Must go for a …

'Jack Perkins! I arrest you in the name of the …
'It's no good Chris. I can't take any …
'Retractors Sister and mop my …
'Can't stand that Eileen. She's an absolute …

'Look out Sergeant! He's got a …
'Well done, Mrs Howard! You have a …
'Missiles? The peace keepers hold the …
'In the name of the father, and the son and of the holy …

Peter Weekley

- What does the title of the poem mean?

- Why are there three dots at the end of each line?

- What different scenes are being described? Write an ending to each line.

- Write a final entry in your note-book. Explain:

  – the point this poem is making

  – how it makes its point

  – how the poem is similar or different to 'Flames'.

- Write your own 'blinding flash' poem about a sudden explosion. Use the same idea of lines of speech which are never finished.

BEING BOTHERED

We watch wars on television. We read about wars in newspapers. We play computer games where people are destroyed at the press of a button.

Killing people can seem like a game. It does not seem to be a part of our real lives. But not many of us see war itself.

BOSNIA TUNE

As you sip your brand of scotch,
crush a **roach**, or scratch your crotch,
as your hand adjusts your tie,
people die.

In the towns with funny names,
hit by bullets, caught in flames,
by and large, not knowing why,
people die.

In small places you don't know
of, yet big for having no
chance to scream or say good-bye,
people die.

People die as you elect
brand new dudes who preach neglect,
self-restraint, etc – whereby
people die.

Too far off to practise love
for thy neighbour/brother **Slav**,
where your **cherubs** dread to fly,
people die.

As you watch the athletes score,
check your latest statement, or
sing your child a **lullaby**,
people die.

Time, whose sharp, blood-thirsty **quill**
parts the killed from those who kill,
will **pronounce** the latter band
as your brand.

Joseph Brodsky

GLOSSARY

Bosnia – country in which there was a war in the 1990s

roach – the end part of a marijuana cigarette

Slav – people of Eastern Europe

cherubs – angels or innocent children

lullaby – song sung to small children to get them to sleep

quill – feather pen

pronounce – judge

A Bosnian woman weeps over her son's coffin, Bosnia 1994

- In 'Bosnia Tune' two words are repeated a lot: 'People die'. Look at the first and sixth stanzas. List the sort of things we do as people are dying in wars.

- Read the last stanza very carefully. The poet writes about two 'tribes' of people. There are those who are 'the killed' and 'those who kill'. Which of these sentences best sums up the poet's view at the end of the poem?

  a) We will all fight in wars and kill people.

  b) By not taking any notice, it is partly our fault that people die. We should do something to stop wars.

  c) We may be killed in wars ourselves.

  d) We should enjoy our lives as much as we can.

- Write your own poem which tells people to care about war. Start your poem like Joseph Brodsky: *'As you sip your ...'*.